A Guide to Puppy Love:

Beginner Breeding

By Virginia Clark

Trade Paperback

Copyright 2015

All Rights Reserved

Library of Congress: 1-2629584861

ISBN 10: 099684371X

ISBN 13: 978-0996843713

Requests for information should be addressed to:

A Vegas Publisher, LLC.

www.avegaspublisher.com

avegaspublisher@yahoo.com

First edition: 2015

Cover Design: Laurie and Fayne Evans

Interior Design: Virginia Clark

Photography furnished by: Virginia Clark

Images provided by: Virginia Clark

DISCLAIMER: Although the author and publisher have made every effort to ensure that the information in this book was correct at press time, the author and publisher do not assume and hereby disclaim any liability to any party for any loss, damage, or disruption caused by errors or omissions, whether such errors or omissions result from negligence, accident, or any other cause.

Printed in the United States of America

To my husband Robert…

My daily inspiration.

Every journey starts with a single step.

-Confucius

Introduction

On my 47th birthday, I was unaware this day I was to embark on the next part of my life's journey. This new journey has filled my life with an abundance of happiness, fulfillment, and reward. My husband surprised me with the best gift I have ever received. He walked in the door with an eight-week-old, bouncy, enthusiastic, perky-eared, black and tan, purebred male German shepherd puppy. I wept with joy and hugged him until he squealed. It was love at first sight. In honor of one of my all-time favorite actors, John Wayne, I named my new "little man," Duke. My husband then added we were going to also get a female German shepherd puppy and would breed them in the future. I was speechless as I pondered the idea. I had sold my company and moved from the East Coast to Nevada with retirement in mind. Boy, was I wrong? Breeding puppies? I had a lot to learn and eagerly went about studying how to become the best breeder I could be.

When Duke was six months old, we bought our pure bred, silky and svelte, black female German shepherd puppy. In honor of Julia Robert's character in one of my favorite movies, *Steel Magnolias*, I named her Shelby. Duke and Shelby bonded instantly and have since remained inseparable. We knew we had the perfect match when the time came to breed.

Once Shelby was of age and in estrus, meaning she was in heat, they successfully mated. When our first litter arrived, I was overwhelmed with emotion as I witnessed the miracle of life appear before my very eyes. Words cannot describe how beautiful it is to watch a puppy enter this world and squeak out the first sounds of life. Get your camera and video ready! The sights and sounds of this glorious moment are forever etched into my mind's eye as they will be in yours.

With every litter whelped, Shelby picked up her first-born puppy and laid it at my feet. It is her gift to me. She looked up at me waiting for praise and then resumed birthing the rest of her puppies. I cry every time she has given me her first puppy. It fills me with pure, unadulterated love.

Granted, all the research I did to prepare myself for our first litter was nothing compared to the actual hands-on experience. Being a first-time breeder, I was filled with concern wondering if I was doing everything right. It was such a satisfying feeling realizing I excelled at rearing our first litter. I trusted my instincts and applied the acquired knowledge from researching all about breeding. It was a lot of hard work, albeit engaging, and with many sleepless nights in the beginning. Once the first litter was re-homed, empty nest syndrome hit me hard. I fell in love with the puppies during their first eight weeks of life while in my care, and when they were gone, I missed them dearly. I could not wait to do it all over again.

I am considered a backyard breeder. Often, the term backyard breeder is spoken with derogatory condemnation, but it does not necessarily mean that everyone who breeds dogs in their home should be considered an unworthy breeder. If you execute good breeding practices, maintain excellent health of your dam, sire and puppies, continually strive to learn more about breeding, and run an honest and ethical operation then you will not take offence at being referred to as a "backyard breeder." You can be proud to be a part of enhancing the German shepherd breed from your home kennel.

After you read this book, you will have to ask yourself: Am I ready to take this journey? Do I possess the gumption and moxie required to excel at breeding? Am I willing to take the first step? If you answer an enthusiastic yes to all of these questions, get ready to embark on a life changing experience filled with an abundance of happiness, fulfillment, and reward. Just follow my lead, and I will walk you through the journey step-by-step.

Duke and Shelby

Table of Contents

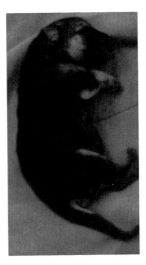 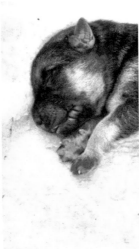  

Chapter 1

Considerations for Starting Your Home Kennel Breeding Business

Operating a dog breeding business is a challenge. You need to learn all aspects of the breeding process in advance to be sure you understand and can appreciate the amount of hard work that is required so you produce healthy puppies while enhancing the quality of the breed. Starting this type of business requires a significant investment of time and effort as well as money for dogs, licensing, veterinarian care, food, and supplies. The business can be rewarding if you love a particular breed and have the knowledge and patience to gradually develop your business.

Based on my experiences, I will focus this discussion specifically on the German shepherd breed, but most of this information can pertain to breeding many other large breeds as well. If there is a kennel in your area where you could volunteer time in trade for mentoring, you will be able to learn firsthand if dedicating yourself to this venture is the right plan for you. Survey your home to be sure you have adequate space indoors for your whelping pen and to be sure you have ample secure outdoor space for your dogs.

After all considerations, if you decide that you want to proceed with breeding large dogs you want to start with purchasing your own male and female as puppies to breed once they are several years of age. It is important to raise your own male and female for breeding to avoid negotiating contracts with other breeders, finding a reliable stud service, or dealing with the shipment of semen and fertility treatments. By owning your own male and female, you are involved with the entire process from mating, through pregnancy, to whelping and caring for the puppies. We will go from the beginning to the end of this process, and I will share with you all I have learned during my professional ongoing career as a German shepherd breeder.

The first step requires checking with your local municipality regarding the laws on operating a home kennel. You need to verify you comply with zoning ordinances. Once you know you will be able to establish a kennel, you can proceed with the search for the puppies: your male, called a sire, and your female, called a dam, that you will breed once they have become of proper age. After you have bought them, you will need to license them, file for your breeders permit, apply for a general business license, and check with your state government to see if you must collect sales tax on your pups when sold. Also, add an addendum to your homeowner's insurance policy providing coverage in the event a person or another dog is injured or attacked while on your property is a good idea.

Duke and Shelby at 4 months old

Duke and Shelby at 2 years old and ready for their first mating

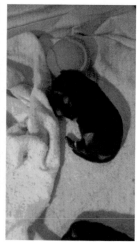

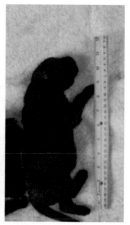

Chapter 2

Selecting Your German Shepherd Female and Male as Puppies

You have given great consideration as to why you want to breed German shepherds. You realize this can be an expensive venture and have the necessary resources to provide for your puppies and those babies they will produce two years down the road. You have studied how to become a proper breeder and have decided you want to invest your effort, time, and money into enhancing the German shepherd breed in your home. You understand this is not a commitment to venture into lightly and are ready to proceed with finding your male and female puppies. So, what is next step?

You want to find the best breeding prospects as possible. Finding a reputable breeder takes time and research. Start by reviewing the breeders listed on the akc.org web site. You may be able to find breeders in your area. If you do not have success locating breeders in your area, then you may have to do some online research for local breeders. You may even find some in your local classified ads. Other avenues to explore are to ask your veterinarian, visit local dog schools, dog groomers, and any other dog related business in your area.

You should try to visit several breeders in your area before making any puppy-buying decisions. Because you are planning to purchase a male and a female puppy, you will want to find two separate breeders and buy your male from one kennel and your female from another. You want to be certain both the male and female come from different bloodlines. This is why it is important to visit American Kennel Club (AKC) registered kennels so you can see the Pedigree Certificates of the dam and sire. This is the best way to know the lineage of your new puppies and to be certain you have healthy, quality stock for breeding in two years.

You will want to ask if the sire and dam that have produced the puppy you are interested in buying have hip and elbow *OFA* numbers to certify they are free of dysplasia. If not certified, have they been x-rayed and what were the results? The *OFA* is the Orthopedic Foundation for Animals, and their mission is to *promote the health and welfare of companion animals through a reduction in the incidence of genetic disease.* Prior to breeding your sire and dam, your veterinarian should be able to perform the tests and x-rays on your male and female pups so you have the proper medical reports and verification indicating your male and female are deemed healthy to reproduce genetically fit litters of puppies.

What to look for at the kennels you visit: Is this kennel clean? If you do not find the environment sanitary such as seeing feces littering the yard, find the puppies lacking in proper kennel care and/or space, see any neglected adult dogs on the premises, and find the breeder avoiding answering your questions, then you should look for another breeder. One simple check to see if he/she is properly caring for the adult dogs and puppies is to look at the water bowls and food bowls. If they show signs of neglect this is not the kennel where you should purchase your new puppy. A sanitary environment promotes healthy dogs.

Keep in mind that once you have bred your sire and dam, you should be answering these same questions when the time comes to find owners for your puppies. Questions you should ask the breeder include:

- ✓ Are the puppies parents certified? Most diseases are inherited, and you want to be sure there are no hip, eye, heart problems, or other diseases that may be passed from the parent to the pups.

- ✓ Ask to see the parents. This is an indication of the size you can expect your puppy to be as an adult. You want to be sure your male and female will grow to be similar in size for breeding compatibility.

- ✓ Do the puppies come with AKC Litter Registration? You must have this certification in order to breed certified AKC puppies.

- ✓ Does the breeder socialize the puppies? Ask for details on how the puppies were socialized. This is important because you do want a well-adjusted puppy when it comes time to re-home.

- ✓ Does the breeder de-worm the puppies? It is common for puppies to be born with worms and deworming is recommended.

- ✓ Will the puppies have an initial vet visit before leaving the kennel? It is recommended that all the puppies have been examined and have received their first set of shots before re-homing. You want to be sure to get a copy of the vet records, and you should ask for copies from all the other puppies in the litter to be sure all the puppies were healthy. Be sure to know when you should schedule the next vet appointment, which should be four weeks from the puppies initial vet visit.

✓ Does the breeder offer a guarantee? In the event that you puppy is sick and the sickness is directly linked to the kennel, how will the breeder address this issue? It is best to know beforehand what the guarantee is.

✓ Does the breeder require you to spay or neuter your puppy by a certain age? This is called limited registration, and some breeders do require spaying or neutering. You need to understand limited registration because you are planning to breed in the future.

✓ Does the breeder offer a bill of sale? Any reputable breeder will present a bill of sale. Information that should be included on the bill of sale should be the date, breeders name and contact information, your name and contact information, the breeders license number, the gender and age of the puppy, the amount paid and marked paid in full, and a notation stating that if you, the new owner, cannot keep the puppy that the breeder will take it back with no financial compensation in return for the puppy.

✓ Is the breeder expecting you to take the puppy before the age of 8 weeks? For proper growth and development, a puppy should not be re-homed before this age.

✓ Will the breeder answer your questions after you have taken your new puppy home? You may have questions and reliable breeders will welcome your call and help answer any questions that may arise.

✓ Ask for references. Follow up with contacting the references and ask about their experiences with the breeder.

You have now found breeders that meet your qualifications and you've bought your new male and female puppies. What is next? Register your puppies with the AKC and get the Certified Pedigree Certificates. You will then raise your puppies, maintain routine vet visits, train the puppies, and enjoy them!

Avoid taking your dogs to dog parks; the grounds of dog parks can be contaminated with disease, parasites, viruses, fleas, and many other unknown variables. You want to keep your dogs as healthy as possible because you intend to breed them at the proper age. If you want to let your dogs run and play, I recommend you go to a secluded open area that may offer a healthier environment for them to enjoy.

Between six months and nine months of age, your female will go into her first heat, called estrus. You do not want to have mating occur at this time. You want your female to be two-years-old before mating. She needs to be fully grown with a mature reproductive system. You can expect estrus to occur every six months from the first estrus. It is important to write down the dates so you are prepared for estrus. The indications of estrus include a bloody discharge, swollen external vulva, and increased urination. She may even be irritable and nervous. I have often been asked how to recognize a swollen vulva and compare it to looking like a tulip in bloom. It is important to keep your male and female separated during estrus to prevent an unwanted pregnancy before your female is of proper age. It is extremely difficult to keep them apart and due diligence on your part is necessary.

If possible, you would find it easier to have your male stay with friends or family until estrus passes. Estrus lasts between two and three weeks, and you know the cycle has ended when the swollen external vulva returns to its normal size. Male dogs can sense a female dog in estrus from over a mile away, so you need to be certain your outdoor space is completely secure.

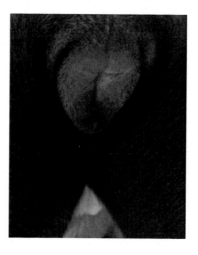

Swollen Vulva

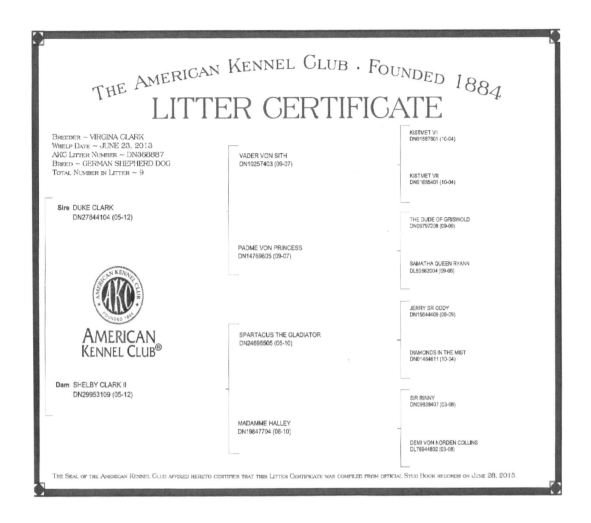

THE AMERICAN KENNEL CLUB · FOUNDED 1884

LITTER CERTIFICATE

BREEDER ~ VIRGINA CLARK
WHELP DATE ~ JUNE 23, 2013
AKC LITTER NUMBER ~ DN368887
BREED ~ GERMAN SHEPHERD DOG
TOTAL NUMBER IN LITTER ~ 9

Sire DUKE CLARK
DN27844104 (05-12)

VADER VON SITH
DN10257403 (09-07)

KISTMET VII
DN01587801 (10-04)

KISTMET VIII
DN01655401 (10-04)

PADME VON PRINCESS
DN14769605 (09-07)

THE DUDE OF GRISWOLD
DN09797208 (09-06)

SAMATHA QUEEN RYANN
DL83662004 (09-06)

AMERICAN KENNEL CLUB®

Dam SHELBY CLARK II
DN29953109 (05-12)

SPARTACUS THE GLADIATOR
DN24696505 (06-10)

JERRY SR CODY
DN15644409 (08-09)

DIAMONDS IN THE MIST
DN01464611 (10-04)

MADAMME HALLEY
DN19847704 (06-10)

SIR RINNY
DN09838407 (03-08)

DEMI VON NORDEN COLLINS
DL76944802 (03-08)

THE SEAL OF THE AMERICAN KENNEL CLUB AFFIXED HERETO CERTIFIES THAT THIS LITTER CERTIFICATE WAS COMPILED FROM OFFICIAL STUD BOOK RECORDS ON JUNE 28, 2013.

AKC Litter Certificate: This is an example of the certificate you would get from The American Kennel Club when you register your litter. This certificate shows the most recent generations in the family tree of the sire and dam. Accompanying this certificate you will receive individual AKC Registration kits for each puppy. Upon the sale of your puppies, you will give a copy of the registration to each new family transferring ownership of the puppy from you to them.

AKC Certified Pedigree Certificate: This is an example of the certificate you would get when you register your male and female puppies you bought for breeding. This certificate shows the past three generations in the family tree. You will get one certificate for your female and one for your male.

Chapter 3

Mating Your Dam and Sire

Time has passed, and your dam and sire are now two-years-old and are ready to mate. All your hard work researching how to become a breeder, finding the right breeder to buy your male and female from as puppies, and all the care put forth raising them has culminated towards the end goal of mating. You now ask, what is next?

Once the bloody discharge begins to appear slightly pink and watery, usually one week into estrus, your female will begin to ovulate, and she will show signs to begin breeding. You will see indications of mating rituals. Your female will be amorous and dance around your male, have frequent urination around the yard to mark territory, and begin to flag her tail to one side to allow your male to mount her. With increased hormonal activity, your male will also exhibit behaviors out of the ordinary during estrus such as licking the female's urine, whining, howling, and he may urinate in the house to mark his territory.

Once the male mounts the female and he has entered her, the process known as a "tie" begins. The vagina will constrict around the shaft of the male's penis and the male's penis, known as the bulbus glandis, swells inside the vagina holding the pair together for ten to twenty minutes while ejaculation takes place. The pair usually turns butt to butt, but sometimes they are side-by-side as well while they remain tied. Once a tie is evident, you should not intervene and try to break up mating; this will cause irreparable damage to both the male and female reproductive organs.

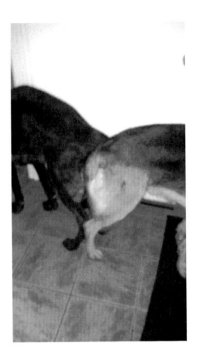

This is a "tie"

You should supervise the ties to keep your male and female calm; you want to be sure the female does not jerk quickly or twist suddenly and injure the penis.

Once the process is complete, they will separate on their own and will groom themselves. The process is exhausting for them, and they will drink plenty of water and sleep afterwards. You need to keep an eye on the male to be sure his penis has retracted back inside like normal. You will find your male and female mating often during estrus; the sperm can last up to five days inside the female, and if you witness the first tie, you need to note the date on the calendar. Count out 63 days from the first tie, and that should be the day the puppies are born, called the "whelp date."

It is not easy to notice if your female is pregnant right away. For the first three weeks, you may not notice any difference at all in her behavior. She may sleep a bit more but other than that, the indications are slight. My female showed one subtle sign at the onset of pregnancy: her nipples began to grow ever so slightly and became slightly pink in color. By the 3rd week though, you will see more defined indications of pregnancy such as increased appetite and thirst, and sleeping more. You will not begin to see an extended abdomen this early into the pregnancy.

After the 3rd week you could go to the vet, have your female examined, and have an ultrasound performed to verify a successful mating; I always knew my female had a successful mating and did not have an ultrasound done.

Once the estrus cycle passed, and I witnessed a successful tie, I did begin to feed my female supplements to her diet, which included raw meat and raw eggs to give her extra protein. Some breeders recommend feeding the dam puppy food throughout the pregnancy to enhance the diet. Your female will eat twice the amount of food she normally consumes while pregnant. Some females may have morning sickness and vomit intermittently during the first few weeks of pregnancy.

By mid-pregnancy, you will begin to see an enlarged abdomen and breast development. You may not notice milk production until the end of the gestation period, but you will notice the enlarged milking glands. The closer your female gets to the whelp date you will notice her sleeping more, and she will exhibit nesting behavior. The term "nesting" refers to her seeking out corners of the house to hide. You may find her scratching at the carpet, digging holes in the yard, and other behaviors you have not seen before. This is a natural instinct to find a place to deliver her pups. Midway through her pregnancy, you should begin to gather the whelping supplies you need and build your whelping pen; this will be discussed in Chapter 4.

Once the whelping pen is built, you should encourage your female to nest in the pen so she feels familiar in the environment by the time the pups arrive. In the beginning, I sat in the whelping pen with my female and petted her so she became comfortable in the pen. By her second litter, she knew this was her zone and would go into the pen on her own to sleep.

Shelby feels right at home in the whelping pen watching over her four-day-old pups

Chapter 4

Supplies

Whelping pen supplies

Whelping pen: Plan for the pen to measure 9 feet long by 7 feet wide. The size may seem large, but when the pups grow, they will require this amount of space. The whelping pen is discussed more in depth in Chapter 12.

Whelping blankets: it is best to have at least 4 to 6 blankets on hand. You will be laundering them regularly and will need a supply to keep in rotation. It is best to use twin-size blankets and not quilts as they do not launder well because of their bulkiness. Also, they do not launder to a sanitized acceptance. Wash the blankets with just a splash of bleach added to the detergent for maximum sanitization.

Heat lamps: Two clamp lights with red 250-watt bulbs. The pups will require additional heat for the first 2 to 3 weeks. After that, they begin to generate their own heat, and you can remove the lamps. Pups need to remain between 85 and 90 degrees for the first five days of life.

Digital thermometer: For use in determining when the pups are expected to arrive, the dam's temperature will drop down to about 98 degrees approximately 12-24 hours prior to whelping.

Free standing thermometer: To measure the temperature of the whelping pen during the puppies first three weeks.

Digital scale: To weigh each puppy.

Measuring tape: To measure the length of each puppy.

Identification supplies

Colored yarn: Plan to have at least nine different colors of yarn to tie around the neck of each puppy for identification.

Litter collars: can be found at pet stores and become handy once their new owners select the pups. Purchase multi-colored collars for identification, and get a pack of ten collars in the adjustable small size.

Cleaning supplies

Six month supply of newspapers: Just save the black print sections, and not the advertisement and feature sections that are made of a non-absorbent paper. You will need this amount of paper for training the puppies to void upon once they begin to eat solid food.

Mop, bucket, broom, dustpan, and garbage bags: You will need these items for proper sanitization of the whelping pen.

Gallon of bleach: Bleach is the recommended product to use for its sanitizing properties. You only need two teaspoons of bleach per gallon of water to disinfect surfaces. Keep a fresh bucket of bleach water near the pen at all times. It is convenient to be on hand to mop unexpected clean ups.

Latex gloves: Two boxes of 100 gloves each should suffice.

Sanitizing gel: For hand sanitization when handling the puppies.

Bathing basin: In the beginning, you will be bathing the pups in the pen, and you will need a basin to wash them. I use a turkey-roasting pan, and it works just fine. Once the pups get bigger, you can graduate them to the sink for daily baths.

Puppy shampoo: For bathing when the pups are four weeks of age.

Nail clippers: For use in keeping their razor-sharp nails clipped.

Feeding supplies

Baby bottle: A necessity if you must hand-feed any puppies.

Syringes: In the event you need to hand feed a pup and using bottle is not effective. Wal-Mart offers these for free in the pharmacy. All you have to do is ask.

Nutritional supplement: In the event you need to prepare formula for the pups, you must have the following ingredients on hand: 8-ounce container of vanilla yogurt, 1 can of evaporated milk (not low fat), 2 egg yolks, and infant vitamins. We will discuss this in Chapter 11.

Baby formula: Buy one small container of powdered formula, which will be served as a nutritional supplement during the third week.

Rice cereal: One box of baby food will be the introduction to solid food.

Puppy food: Plan on 50 pounds of dry premium puppy food for starters.

Milk Bones@ biscuits: Have a box of small Milk Bones@ on hand; as the pups grow they enjoy them as a treat.

Litter feeding bowl: Specifically designed stainless steel bowl for feeding a litter of pups. This can be found in pet stores.

Large water bowl: As the pups grow, they will drink a lot of water and need a large stainless steel bowl.

Medical supplies

Hemostats: For clamping umbilical cords before cutting the cord in the event the mother is unable to perform the task.

Children's scissors: To cut the umbilical cord after clamping.

Infant nasal aspirator: For removing amniotic fluid from the puppies nose and throat if the dam is unable to do this.

KY Jelly: To lubricate the thermometer for rectal temperature readings and for use when assisting with the delivery process.

Rubbing alcohol: To clean supplies.

Phone numbers: Have your veterinarian's phone number readily available in the event of an emergency. If the office does not provide 24-hour services then also include an emergency veterinarian phone number in the event your emergency falls outside regular office hours.

Toys

Plan to have soft, plush toys on hand for when the pups grow. Avoid toys with any removable parts such as eyes, noses, and squeakers so the pups do not choke. Plush toys should be laundered daily. Other toys can include balls, ropes, and the best toy of all is an empty water bottle with the cap and label removed; the pups go crazy for such a simple item.

Camera

If you do not own a digital camera, you should consider getting one. You will want to document the journey from birth through adoption of your puppies by taking daily pictures and videos. Uploading your pictures and videos online offers perspective new owners of your puppies' valuable insight on the growth, development, and care your puppies receive.

  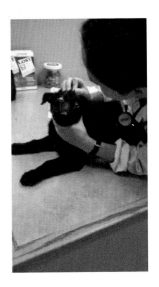

Chapter 5

Stages of Labor

<u>Onset of Labor:</u>

Pregnancy in dogs last approximately 62 to 64 days. One week before the due date, begin to take the dam's rectal temperature daily. Lubricate with KY jelly, insert the thermometer about an inch into the rectum, and wait for the reading. Her temperature should be between 101° and 102.5° Fahrenheit. When the pet's temperature drops below 100° F, she should deliver the pups within twenty-four hours. A week before whelping, give your female a bath. If you have a long hair female, trim the hair around the vulva and nipples.

Resting during onset of labor

<u>Stage One of Labor:</u>

During the first stage of labor, the cervix begins to dilate, and uterine contractions begin. These contractions are painful. She will appear uncomfortable, restless, and may pace and pant. She probably will not eat, and she may even vomit. This is the longest stage of labor. It generally lasts six to eighteen hours. By the end of this period, her cervix will have completely dilated for the puppies to pass. During this time, keep the mother's environment quiet and calm and do not leave her unattended.

Stage one of labor

Stage Two of Labor:

Plan to stay with the dam for the duration of delivery. During the second stage of labor, uterine contractions become stronger. The placental water sack breaks, and a light colored fluid passes. Placentas are expelled after each puppy arrives. The average litter size for German shepherds is eight puppies, and they usually appear every half-hour to an hour after the first one is delivered. As each one arrives, the mother will instinctively tear away the sac, which is called the "amniotic membrane," chew off the umbilical cord, lick the puppy clean, and stimulate the puppy to breathe. It is important to let the mother do this because it is the beginning of the bonding process. The mother will eat the afterbirths. If she does not tear away the sac and lick the pups to stimulate respiration, you should help tear the sac open, clear all fluid away from the pup's nose and mouth using the infant nasal aspirator, and gently rub the puppy on its chest to stimulate breathing. You may need to assist with cutting the umbilical cord using the children's scissors in your supply kit. You may also have to assist with helping a puppy through the birth canal by very gently pulling in a downward motion. You should keep a bowl of water in the whelping pen for the exhausted mother to drink. Bring the bowl to her, and take it away when she is done.

Stage two of labor: a puppy is being delivered

Stage two of labor: removing the amniotic membrane

Stage two of labor: beautiful puppy just moments old

Stage Three of Labor:

Once all the puppies have been born, the female enters this third stage of labor during which time the uterus contracts fully, expelling any remaining placenta, blood, and fluid. You know all the puppies have been delivered with this indicator. The mother will eat everything she has expelled which helps to stimulate milk production.

Post Labor:

At this point, the mother is exhausted. She will need to relieve herself and want to stretch. Give her a few minutes to go outside, walk around the yard, get a drink of water, and perhaps get something to eat. I always reward my female with praise and few bites of raw chicken. She is usually not hungry for a few hours after delivering her puppies, but does need steady nourishment, and I continue to offer her bites of food until she goes to her food bowl on her own. While she is away from her puppies, you should change the soiled blankets with clean blankets and mop up areas that may be unsanitary. I use this time to clean my female up a bit before she goes back to nurse her puppies.

The newborns do not generate their own heat and can develop life threatening hypothermia during the first weeks of life. The puppies begin to generate their own heat and develop the shiver reflex at around three weeks of age.

Turn on both of the heat lamps to warm the whelping pen and avoid drafts near there. Place the free standing thermometer on the floor of the pen near the puppies and maintain a temperature between 85 ° and 90 ° for the next seven days.

During the second week, maintain the temperature between 80 °and 85 °. During the third week, maintain the temperature between 75 ° and 80 °. The temperature during the fourth through eighth week should remain between 70 ° and 75 °. The heat lamps should be placed 4 feet to 5 feet above the puppies so you gently warm them.

Puppies just moments old: resting under heat lamps

Identify each puppy right away by tying a piece of different colored yarn around the neck of each puppy. Document the length and weight of each puppy. To easily weigh the puppies line a small container (such as a food storage container) with a washcloth. Place the container on the digital scale and weigh. Now place a puppy into the container to weigh. Deduct for the weight of the empty container, and you will have the accurate weight of the puppy. Continue to document the length and weight of each puppy daily for the next two weeks. This will give you a good indication that the puppies are growing properly and receiving enough nourishment. On average, puppies will double its weight by one-week-old followed by a consistent 5% to 10% increase daily. Next, you will need to identify the gender of each puppy. The female puppy will have a very small leaf like shape between her back legs near the anus; this is the vagina. The male puppy will have a very small dot near the belly; this is the penis.

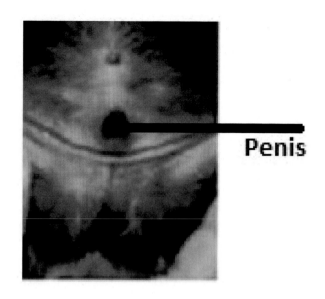

Penis

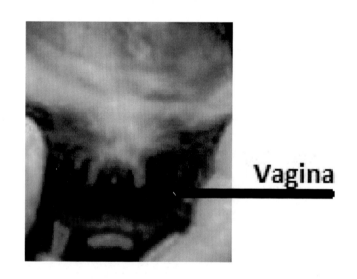

Vagina

The day after whelping you should take your dam to the vet to get a post-partum checkup. Your vet will feel her uterus to make sure all the pups and placentas have been expelled, as well as put her on an antibiotic to prevent an infection from taking hold.

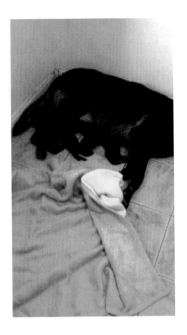

Post labor with pups: nursing at twelve-hours-old

 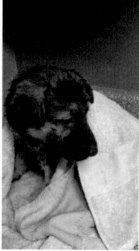 

Chapter 6

Week-by-Week Growth and Development and Your Role as Midwife

Shelby whelping her first pup from Litter #4: she proudly brings her baby to me:

https://www.youtube.com/watch?v=uSms0anBF7Q

Pups are 4 days old:

https://www.youtube.com/watch?v=CmHz3ODmTwY

Pups at one-week-old:

https://www.youtube.com/watch?v=3XYnFGikwK4

Week 1

- This is a very busy time for you, and you will not get much sleep. The mother and the newborn puppies are fragile and will need your help around the clock. I sleep in my recliner beside the whelping pen so I can be available at all times. You want to be sure that the puppies are warm and fed regularly.

- The puppies will nurse about every 15 to 20 minutes during this week; this duration extends as the puppies grow older. You need to monitor the nursing so all the puppies receive ample supplies of milk. Help with lining up the pups to nurse and be available every time the puppies need to nurse. You want to be sure the mother does not accidentally squish the puppies, and you need to rotate pups for equal nursing. Monitor the larger pups from nursing more while some of the smaller pups may be nursing less by getting pushed aside. When sleeping, wake smaller pups to nurse separately to get extra nourishment.

- In between feeds, the puppies will sleep. They may squirm and wiggle around and unintentionally get away from the heat. Be sure you keep the puppies under the heat lamps at all times. The greatest danger a puppy will face during the first week of life is if they get cold, referred to as "chilling." To test if a puppy is chilled you have to feel the tongue. If the tongue is cold to the touch then warm him/her immediately because this could be life threatening. You need to warm him/her gradually and evenly. The best way to do this is to place the puppy under the heat lamp and rotate it from side-to-side so the puppy is being warmed evenly. You could also wrap it in a towel and hold it in your hands until the puppy is warm. Under no circumstances should a chilled puppy nurse until warmed as this could be fatal.

- The mother will clean her pups and lick their bottoms. This stimulates the puppies to void, and the mother will instinctively clean their urine and feces.

- The mother is very protective of her babies and may not want the sire in the pen. She will be selective on what people can enter the pen. This is her space, and she will let you know when the father and other people can be near the pups.

- It is best to let the mother in and out of the pen as needed. She will try to jump over the walls of the pen to gain entry or exit. She may injure herself or her pups in the process. It is best to avoid letting the mother have her own free access into and out of the pen, and I base this solely on our own experiences. The first whelping pen we built allowed the mother freedom of access allowing her to come and go as she pleased. However, she kept trying to bring her pups to me or hiding them in the house thus putting the babies in jeopardy. For their safety, adjustments had to be made to the whelping pen where she had to be let in or out as needed.

- Sanitize the pen: This is a daily or even multi-daily task, which includes changing the bedding, and sweeping and mopping the floor. The puppies are only as healthy as their environment. A sanitized whelping pen is a priority at all times. The older the puppies get, the busier you will be with sanitizing the area.

- During the first week, visit the akc.org website to register your litter. Within two weeks, you should receive your AKC litter registration kit and all the required documentation, which you will give to the new owners of your pups at the time of re-homing. There is a nominal fee to register your litter. If you have not already done so, this would also be a good time to register yourself as a breeder while visiting the AKC website. You could place a classified ad on the site to sell your puppies. The AKC website is a valuable resource, and you should browse the site to learn about a variety of informative subjects.

- Document daily weight and length of each pup to be sure they are growing at the proper rate.
- Take pictures daily and post on your blog and social media sites.

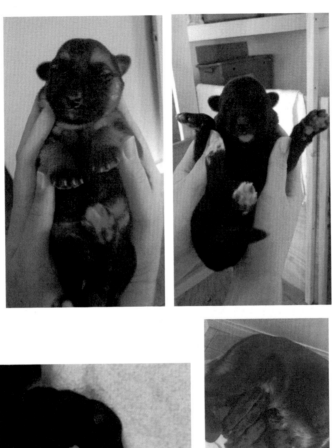

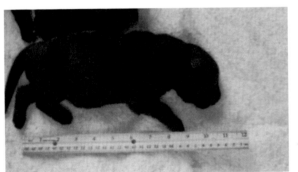

One-week-old puppies

Week 2

Pups at two-weeks-old:

https://www.youtube.com/watch?v=cD3Woa1lrws

- Feeding begins to stretch out to about one hour between feeds. This is around the clock, and you still need to be a part of this process with helping line them up so they can all nurse equally. You need to monitor the larger ones, remove them from the nipple after a reasonable time, and put the smaller ones on the nipple. As previously mentioned, the smaller ones usually are squeezed out during nursing. You want to be sure you have equal nutrition to all of them with a focus on the smallest of the litter. You will notice that near the end of the 2nd week, the pups make their way to the mother more easily by squirming and trying to pull themselves to her. Some try to stand at this time.

- By the end of the 2nd week the eyes will begin to open and hearing will develop.

- Mother will continue to clean up after her babies.

- The pups will sleep a lot in between feeds.

- Mother may now allow the sire and others to enter the pen.

- Pups should have doubled their weight by the end of the 2nd week.

- Be careful when entering the pen, because the pups tend to wiggle their way under the blankets, and you cannot see them. You don't want to accidentally step on a pup. It is a good idea to always do a head count when entering the pen to be sure all pups are accounted for and not hidden beneath the bedding.

- Continue daily sanitization of the bedding and floor of the pen.

- Document daily weight and length of each pup to be sure the puppies are growing at the proper rate. By the end of Week 2, you can discontinue weighing and measuring as long as you see proper weight gain and growth.

- Take pictures daily and post on your blog and social media sites.

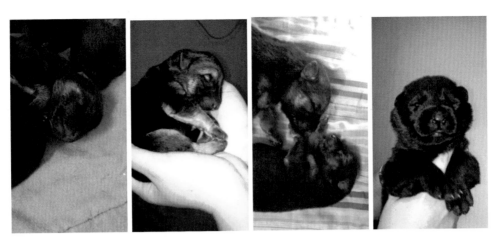

Two-week-old puppies: notice the eyes beginning to open in the right side picture

Week 3

Pups at three-weeks-old:

https://www.youtube.com/watch?v=PiA33PvZ3GI

- Feeding stretches to about one hour and 15 to 30 minutes. Continue the round-the-clock feeding assistance.
- Mother continues to clean up after the pups, but now it is time to also begin mopping more often and changing the blankets as needed. The pups are urinating and defecating with more frequency.
- The puppies will begin standing and walking during this week. They will become quite active and chatty at this time. Teeth will have broken the gum line.
- During the third week, you can begin to bathe the puppies' daily using lukewarm water only. Do not use shampoo at this time. Once the pen is sanitized and blankets have been changed, sit in the pen and wash the pups. Be sure to have towels and washcloth on hand before baths. The pups enjoy being introduced to warm water, and you will find it has a calming effect. This is pleasurable for the pups, and is a good bonding experience between you and them. Bathing is also beneficial to the pups because they will avoid the fear of water at an early age. Dry the pups well, and keep the heat lamps on to further dry them so they are not chilled.

- Towards the end of the third week the puppies will demand more milk from the mother because they are rapidly growing. Begin to introduce a nutritional supplement to the pups using baby formula. Using a small pan, such as a pie pan, works well and the pups need to be introduced to the pan and shown what to do. They do not know how to drink yet, and this helps the learning process. One pup at a time, quickly dip their nose into the liquid. They will begin to lick and begin to get the idea. It is a good idea to let the mother drink the supplement in front of the pup so they watch and learn this new process. Soon the puppies will be on solid food and drinking water, and they will no longer need baby formula. The pups will continue to nurse while enjoying the addition of a nutritional supplement to their diet.
- The pups will sleep a lot.
- Continue the daily sanitization routine.
- Mother may allow other people near her pups.
- Take pictures daily and post on your blog and social media sites.

First baths at three-weeks-old

First nutritional supplements at three-weeks-old

Week 4

Pups at 22 days old going outside for the first time:

https://www.youtube.com/watch?v=x5rhpaHzKJ0

Pups at four-weeks-old:

https://www.youtube.com/watch?v=51dr9Rbp0Bg

- Things really begin to change during Week 4. You will introduce solid food to them. The first step to introducing solid food is to begin by mixing a small bowl of baby rice cereal with some of the baby formula. You want the consistency to be a bit loose so they can easily swallow. Sit and hold one of them at a time and spoon-feed the cereal with very tiny amounts of cereal on the tip of the spoon. Continue feeding each one until he/she has eaten a teaspoon worth of cereal. You do not want to over-feed the puppy nor rush the process. Gently introduce solid food, and let the puppy digest the cereal with ease. One of the purposes of the colored yarn is to make sure you feed each of them, and no one is left out. After an hour has passed, follow this process again and continue to do so for the remainder of the day. During the course of the first day, the baby cereal will have made its way through the entire digestive tract, and they will void a different, more solid stool than usual, which is what we are looking for. Once they have eaten and voided and you experience no problems with digestion, you can prepare the baby food and leave it in a small pan in the pen. They will instinctively go to the food and begin to eat without needing to be spoon-fed.

Once the puppies have finished the one box of baby cereal, you are ready to transition to puppy food. A premium dry puppy food can be served to the pups using the litter-feeding pan. You will find that the first few times you serve the food it would be best to have the food soaked in water until soft. It takes about thirty minutes for the food to absorb enough water to be ready for feeding. Arrange the pups around the pan so they understand this is their food. After the first few days of serving the food softened in water, begin to serve the food—as it is right out of the bag. Plan to keep food available at all times, because the pups have varied hunger, and you want them to eat when they are hungry.

- The pups will be drinking water now, and you want to be sure to have fresh water available at all times. I find it handy keeping an empty milk jug filled with water near the pen to easily refill the water bowl as needed.

- With solid food introduced into the diet, the mother will slowly begin to wean the pups from nursing. The pups will still nurse but with less frequency. You will still need to check on the pups during the night to clean up the pen and to nurse, but by the end of Week 4 you will only need to check on them three to four times during the night.

- During this time you may find the mother wanting to go into the pen after eating. She will regurgitate her meal for the pups to feed on. This is a normal and natural process for the mother to nurture her pups. Be sure to feed the mother again, and be sure to keep a watchful eye on them while they consume the food the mother has given them in the event they may choke on her food.

- Now that solid food has been introduced, it's time to begin to paper train. They are urinating and defecating with even more frequency. This is the time to sanitize the pen as often as needed. This is where keeping a mop and bucket of bleach water on hand becomes convenient, and be sure to change the water often. You will also be changing the blankets more often. Paper-training techniques are discussed in Chapter 13.

- During this week, you will see the pups' personalities awaken. They will become quite playful, and their motor skills will become more developed. This is a good time to introduce toys for them to play with.

- Depending on the climate, the pups will be able to go outside for brief outings. This is a very exciting time for the pups as they begin to explore the outdoors. Always supervise their outdoor activities for their safety.

- The puppies will be soiled more often and will require at least one bath daily, but be prepared to bathe more often as needed. This is the time to begin bathing them using puppy shampoo. Be sure to rinse the pups well and towel dry well to keep them from being chilled.

- They will also be awake longer. They will still sleep a lot but with less frequency as in previous weeks.

- It is quite common for German shepherd puppies to be reserved prior to birth. People love this breed and are willing to wait for their pups. During Week 4 you can allow the reserved pups to be selected. Once the new owner makes their selection, place a color-coded collar on their choice for identification and remove the colored yarn. Be certain to keep accurate documentation on both the pup and the new owner. Finding perspective owners is discussed in Chapter 8.

- During Week 4 you should gather a collective feces sample to take to the vet to be tested for worms, parasites, Giardia, and any other possible contaminants. A collective sample means taking a small piece of stool from several pups and combining them into one sample.

- If the collective sample tests negative, then all the babies and their mother will test negative. Results usually take one day. The vet will call to confirm the findings and prescribe necessary medication if needed.

- Their nails will have grown and are razor sharp. To provide comfort for the nursing mother, you may need to carefully trim the nails.

- During Week 4 you should call your veterinarian to schedule the pups 7 to 8 week wellness visit and to begin the first series of shots. By calling in advance, you will most likely be guaranteed a date and time that best suits your schedule.

- Continue the sanitizing routine and remember to clean the water and food bowls and toys as well.

- Take pictures daily and post on your blog and social media sites.

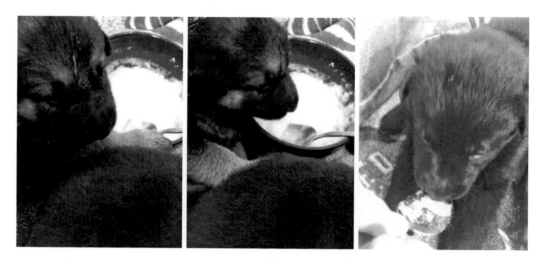

Four-weeks-old and eating baby rice cereal for the first time

At four weeks old, pups are eating puppy food from the litter feeding pan. Notice some of the pups fell asleep in the bowl while eating. The color-coded collars indicate they've already been reserved by their new owners

Four-weeks-old when paper training begins

Four-weeks-old and loving the toys

Four-weeks-old and going outside for the first time

Four-weeks-old and bathing with puppy shampoo

Meeting adoptive parents at four-weeks-old

More adoptive parents – Four-weeks-old photo ops.

Week 5 and 6

Pups at five-weeks-old:

https://www.youtube.com/watch?v=zdREY9YXKNY

Pups at six-weeks-old:

https://www.youtube.com/watch?v=kiToVD9ZlmY

- The pups have become ravenous and will be eating quite a bit more. By now they should be eating dry puppy chow, drinking more water and the need to nurse from the mom will be reduced. The mother will still nurse but with less frequency, and she may continue to regurgitate her dinner for them to consume. The pups will also enjoy nibbling on small Milk Bone@ biscuits.

- With increased appetites, comes increased voiding. You will need to clean the pen more often and this includes during the night as well. For the health of the pups, it is important to keep the pen as sanitized as much as possible. Continue your sanitization routine but with more frequency.

- The pups begin to play hard towards the end of Week 4 and into Week 5. They will take fewer naps and when they do finally fall asleep, they'll drop right where they are and will sleep for a longer duration.

- They will enjoy going outside more often. They are inquisitive and mischievous at this age and require supervision while outside. Be certain that the climate is not too hot or too cold during their time outdoors.

- Bathe them at least once daily and sometimes more than once a day. They will roll and tumble around while playing. They may roll in their waste so keeping them clean is imperative.

- The pups' ears will begin to stand. It takes several months before the ears stand tall and straight permanently.

- Trim nails if necessary.

- Mentally, the pups begin to develop at a rapid rate. They begin to recognize a few simple words such as "out," "eat," and "no." Talking and socializing with to the pups encourages them to know these simple commands. The communication is welcoming to them because their minds begin to absorb knowledge at a very young age. Scientific studies have shown dogs that receive early proper socialization actually have increased brain mass. They are also better at problem solving, and become enjoyable, intelligent companions. In addition, they want to learn and are hungry for knowledge.

- Take pictures daily and post on your blog and social media sites.

Chow time with pups at five-weeks-old

Pups recognize the word "out" at five-weeks-old.

Pups at six-weeks-old and enjoy playing outside.
At this age some of the pups' ears begin to stand up.

Week 7 and 8

Pups at seven-weeks-old:

https://www.youtube.com/watch?v=fdqbPFYRZ-g

- Week 7 through 8 will be their most noticeable period of rapid growth and development. They will be getting stronger, solid weight gain, taller, be more playful and quite active. They will also be noisy! The brown and tan colors will become more defined by now, and the colors will continue to develop until they are about one-year-old. Care for them will remain the same as in the previous Weeks of 5 and 6.

- During Week 7 through Week 8, you can take them to the vet for their scheduled examination and their first set of shots. Read the requirements with your Breeder Permit. Some municipalities require your puppies to be micro-chipped before re-homing. Plan for safe transport: two adults should accompany the pups to the vet. It is best to let them outdoors for ½ hour prior to leaving so they can relieve themselves, run around, and burn off excess energy. When the vet visit is complete, ask for copies of the examination, shot records, and micro chipping records. You need one copy for each pup and one copy for your own records. The car ride and vet visit can be a bit overwhelming for the pups. For you too. They will be tired when they return to their pen and will sleep for an extended period. Get ready! They will return to their normal playful selves after a nap.

- Now that Week 8 has arrived, plan for the pups to be re-homed. After all the hard work raising and caring for them pups, it is time say good-bye. In their best interest, don't let them go home before Week 7. It is best to schedule pick-up times that do not overlap so that you, each pup, and his or her new families can spend a few minutes together during the transition. This is a good time to discuss the pup, the vet visit, answer any questions that may arise, and to present the AKC registration documents and vet records to the new owner. Your bill of sale should accompany each pup and should include the date, your complete contact information, the new owners complete contact information, your breeder permit number, and marked paid in full.

- Take pictures daily and post on your blog and social media sites.
- Once all of them have been re-homed you should sanitize all the bedding, food and water bowls, toys, and anything else the pups came in contact with prior to packing away for use with the next litter.

Hi! Ho! Hi! Ho! Off to the vet we go!

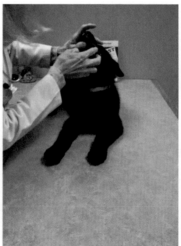

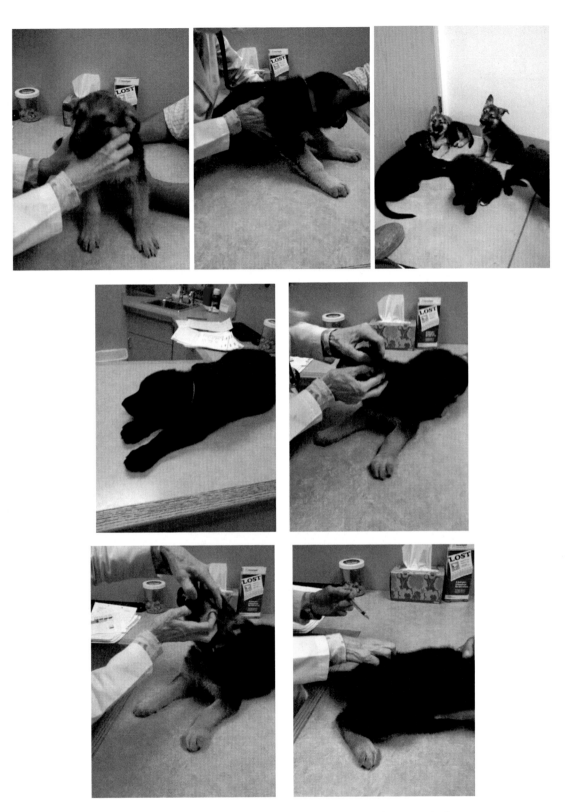

Eight-weeks-old: First vet first examination and shots.

I'm eight-weeks-old and going to a new home.

Chapter 7

Marketing Your Puppies

Breeding your German shepherds is a business. You will need to find good families who will be interested in a permanent adoption, not a foster home. Your puppies will be an integral part of their families. How do you find these worthy families? There are many ways to find good families, and you need to decide how you would like to proceed:

- Word of mouth is a great way to start.
- Place an ad on the AKC.org web site, which validates you as a breeder, but that may not be enough exposure to reach potential local buyers in your area.
- Place a classified ad in your local newspaper.
- Leave flyers to post at your veterinarian's office, at pet stores, at pet groomers, at dog obedience schools, visit your local K9 Corp if your locality trains police dogs, and any other dog-related businesses in your area.
- Collaborate with other breeders in your area.

Personally, I have found some of those avenues of exposure to be less than effective to suit my needs. It can be costly to run advertisements in publications. Also, some undesirables have responded to those advertisements and have expressed interest in adoption but didn't pass the screening process.

You want your puppies to go to good homes so be very selective exposing yourself and the babies to people who may not suitable buyers. You should not advertise your puppies on Craigslist. There are unscrupulous people out there preying on unsuspecting, innocent advertisers and seek to purchase or steal puppies for seedy, illegitimate purposes. You do not want one of your babies ending up in a puppy mill or used as bait or as a fighter in underground dogfight operations.

I use Guerilla Marketing strategies via social media networking. You may find some of these ideas work well for your marketing plan. The method has proven to be highly efficient and is cost effective in reaching my target audience. It takes an investment of time and innovation. In fact, people will wait up to a year in advance to adopt one of our puppies, and it is common for all our puppies to be reserved prior to conception because they follow the activity I post on my social media sites. The whelping and raising of the puppies becomes easier when I do not have to worry about dividing my attention between finding perspective owners while multitasking and caring for the puppies. Of course, it is helpful that I have become known for being an honest and reputable breeder, but that comes with time and by building relationships with people one puppy at a time and one litter at a time.

The idea came to me to use the Internet to market our yet unborn puppies online when we got our own male and female as puppies at eight weeks of age. I never had the opportunity to see Duke and Shelby grow from the moment they were born, which I would have loved. My first memories began once they were adopted and home with us. I thought then, several years before breeding them, that when the time came I would document every litter we had so everyone could see their puppies enter the world and prospective families could watch them grow until the time came to enter their forever homes. One time when we took a litter to the vet for their first check-up, the doctor told me that in all her years of practice that I was the only person she met that documented the journey of the puppy's life. She said it was an original concept and wondered why other breeders do not do this.

With that said, I solely advertise my German shepherd breeding business online. I have built a steady following through my Blog, on my Facebook page, YouTube channel, Google +, and Pinterest. Currently, I have over 130,000 followers between these sites. The secret lies within the content I post in my news feeds, which captures the attention of people who chose to follow my sites. I find that the social profile I developed to be an invaluable tool in the marketing of the puppies. Let me share my process:

I first developed my online presence with pictures and videos of my adult German shepherds. I wanted people to see how beautiful and healthy the dam and sire are. I announced in advance when mating was expected. I regularly updated the progress and included new pictures and videos daily. Over time, I have developed a caring reputation and people contact me to reserve one of our puppies based on my website content.

When the whelp date arrives, I begin to document the journey of each litter from birth through adoption. Daily pictures and videos are posted on my sites so people can log on and virtually watch the growth and development of the puppies. I want transparency and achieve this via daily posts. Once the puppies are old enough for the new owners to come make their selection I place a color-coded ID collar on their pup, and they can clearly see which puppy is theirs in the pictures and on the videos. This allows them to feel included in the puppy process, and it's exciting every time they log onto my sites and see the updates of their new family member. I index the litters on my social media sites, include customer testimonials, and post the many pictures that everyone sends me as their puppies grow into adults. This interaction binds us into a community of true GSD lovers by collectively sharing our passion of the German shepherd breed.

Most importantly, this visual data creates an "aww," moment that no family looking to adopt can ignore. I feel it myself every time we have a whelp. They are precious, busy, fun, mischievous, and become wonderful family members.

Building your blog should be the first site you establish. There are many free blogging platforms to select from and examples of blog sites include WordPress.com, Blog.com, and Blogger.com, where my blog is located: http://akc-german-shepherd-pups-for-sale.blogspot.com/. Visit this site to see the content I have posted and get an indication of the creative material I find engaging for others to view. Once you have established your blog, you can copy and paste your information and your unique website link, called an URL, on other social media sites, which will drive traffic to your pages and develop interest in your breeding skills and your puppies.

You need to reach your target market in order to be found easily online, and you should specifically locate German shepherd sites within your area where like-minded individuals gather. People will not know your online presence exists if you do not share your information with them. You want people to find your information quickly and the more you share your link, the more exposure you will receive thus increasing your opportunity to be located easily by people. Common keyword searches in search engines include such words as: German shepherds, German shepherd puppies, German shepherd pups, German shepherd breeders, etc.

Because German shepherd is often misspelled, be sure to purposely misspell shepherd as "shepard" in your own searches. You would be surprised how often the proper spelling of shepherd is incorrectly spelled. When placing your link online, each keyword search you perform should include your location so you can target people within your vicinity where you will likely be selling your puppies. See the example below with my Facebook page name.

The next online presence to establish is on Facebook where over one billion active monthly users socially engage. Give your page a direct name where you can be easily found. Avoid cute names like Cuddly Puppies for Sale, as an example, because the likelihood of people finding you will be slim to none. Any person in my area looking for German shepherd puppies can quickly and easily find me when searching Facebook for my pet services by using direct, basic keywords. Visit my page to see the content posted: https://www.facebook.com/AkcGermanShepherdPupsForSaleNearLasVegasNv.

When setting up your Blog and Facebook page, do not publicly include your specific house address. Instead just put down your street name or basic locality.

You do not want people knocking at your door without a scheduled appointment nor do you want to be a target for strangers looking for an opportunity to perhaps steal your dam, sire, or puppies.

This is referred to as "pet flipping," and it happens more often than people realize. German shepherds are in the top ten most frequently stolen breeds because they demand top dollar. Once you screen potential people interested in one of your puppies, then privately provide your address. The same applies to publicly posting your phone number to avoid getting phone calls at undesirable hours. Anyone interested in contacting you for information about your puppies can send you a private message, and your information can remain confidential until you decide to provide it. You should include your Breeder License number on your sites, and you may find that the instructions you receive with your license requires you to do so.

After you have established a Blog and Facebook page and you know your unique web presence addresses, you can order business cards with this information on them. I order my business cards from Vistaprint.com. It is an easy site to navigate, and you can custom design your cards.

Visatprint.com often has free offers available where you can order 250 cards and just pay for shipping and handling charges.

Be sure to include your Breeder License number on your business cards. Always keep a supply of cards with you so you can pass them out to anyone who expresses an interest in one of your puppies.

68

Chapter 8
The Adoption Process

I carefully select potential buyers by asking many questions. Their responses to my questions helps define if this is a person worthy of adopting one of our puppies, knowing they will provide a kind and loving home. I encourage potential buyers to meet me, meet the dam and sire, and develop a personal relationship. That is of paramount concern when I'm looking for good families to adopt a puppy. I also want to see how my own German shepherds react to these individuals. I trust my adult dogs' instinctual responses towards people. They are very intuitive, and their reaction tells me a great deal about others. Such screening questions include but are not limited to:

- Why do you want a German shepherd?
- Do you have experience with raising a large dog?
- Do you live in a house or apartment?
- Do you have a fenced yard or will the dog be chained?
- How many hours a day will the dog be left alone?
- Do you have children?
- What is your occupation?
- Do you have other dogs?
- Can you provide references?

Once a person passes the screening process, I will allow the puppies to be viewed and selected. The puppies should be at least four-weeks-old before allowing strangers to handle them. Place the dam and sire outside before allowing viewing of the puppies. The dam will be very protective and will not allow strangers near her pups if she is not separated from them. The selection process is delicate. You want the potential buyers to make a choice that best suits their needs and at the same time, you want to streamline the process so the mother is not separated from her pups for an extended time. She instinctively knows strangers are near her babies, and she wants to be in the pen guarding them. So it is imperative you do not spend too much time handling the puppies and reunite them with the mother and her brood as quickly as possible.

You want to be sure the puppies are not exposed to contaminants. Ask anyone handling the puppies to clean their hands with sanitizing gel. Also, shoes should be removed in the event the soles are contaminated. After selecting which puppy they want to adopt, identify each puppy with their own unique color-coded ID collar so there are no mix-ups at the time of re-homing. Be certain to document the selection, share contact information, collect a deposit to solidify the purchase, and give the potential buyer a receipt. The buyer should know the re-home date in advance so they can prepare their homes, buy supplies, and be ready for the day their pup goes home. I always encourage picture taking once the puppy has been selected. This is a very exciting time in their lives, and the new owners will proudly show their family and friends the newest addition to their family. With their permission, you should take pictures to post on your Blog and Facebook page for others to see. It is contagious…once people see puppies being selected and see the happy new owners with their puppies, the more interest is generated in your available puppy supply.

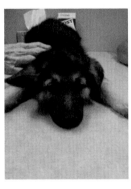  

 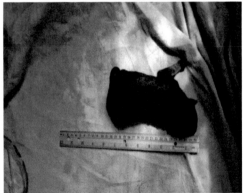 

Chapter 9

Adoption Fees and Collecting a Deposit

Deciding what to charge for an adoption fee is a bit of an enigma. Do a bit of research on the going price in your locality for an AKC registered German shepherd puppy in order to offer a reasonable asking price. Different regions of the United States offer AKC German shepherd puppies for different rates. The East Coast may charge less than the West Coast, for example. You may find multiple breeders of German shepherd puppies in a large geographic area where supply and demand can vary the price. There are other factors to consider when researching prices. Such considerations include, but are not limited to:

- Champion lines are more expensive than non-champion lines.
- Varied bloodlines can affect the price.
- AKC registered purebred German shepherd puppies are more expensive than unregistered purebred German shepherd puppies.
- If you plan to ship your puppy to a different locality then the cost of shipping a puppy will have to be taken into consideration. I do not ship my pups.
- OFA Certified puppies will be more expensive than non-certified puppies.
- Take into consideration how much money you invested into raising your puppies. Accurate record keeping of expenses is helpful in making this determination.
- In the end, you will decide what a reasonable adoption fee should be, and you should remain flexible with this number. A base fee for consideration is $1000.

Accepting a firm deposit fee is essential. To further encourage serious individuals when adopting one of our puppies, I ask for a non-refundable $100 deposit. I make this policy clear upfront and have not had objections from interested buyers.

  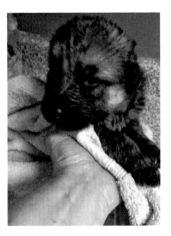

Chapter 10

What to Expect from Your Female Post Adoption:

How Often to Breed

Neither dam nor sire behaves differently once the puppies have all been re-homed. They carry on about their business in usual fashion and adjust to a puppy-free existence. The mother will begin to regain her normal figure, and the mammary glands will dry up and shrink somewhat. She will shed quite a bit of hair at this point, and you will need to give her deep brushing twice a day for several weeks to help rid her of the hair that will come out at steady rates. Continue to supplement her diet with raw meat so she replenishes nutrients that were depleted during her pregnancy and while nursing.

It will not be long before the next estrus cycle begins again. Typically, the female will go into estrus every six months. If you look back on your calendar to the date of the mating and count out six months, you will realize just how quickly the next estrus cycle returns. You need to read the terms and conditions of your Breeder Permit to comply with your local breeding laws. Some permits limit breeding to once a year. Non-compliance could revoke your license, and you could be penalized with a fine.

The health of your female should be taken into consideration if you decide to breed her with back-to-back litters if your permit allows you to do so.

There are two different scientific studies on how often to breed your female, and neither study is conclusively right or wrong:

- The first is to breed back-to-back litters, and retire your female when she is young.
- The second is to skip every other heat cycle, and retire your female when she is older.

The advantage of breeding back-to-back litters is that it is easier on the dams' body to get in shape and stay in shape for pregnancy thus avoiding hormonal ups and downs that are associated with breeding once a year. Retiring your female and having her spayed after four litters means she will still be young, healthy, and active for many years to come. This is my favored choice for breeding.

The disadvantage of breeding once a year is her advanced age after whelping four litters, the hormonal roller coaster she will experience, and the difficulty of keeping the dam and sire separate during estrus. It is easier said than done controlling Mother Nature during estrus, and you may have to remove the sire from your home for several weeks until the heat cycle is finished. It is also difficult on the older female to recover when it does come time for her to be spayed.

Most importantly, and I cannot reiterate this enough: the health and well-being of your female should be your first and foremost consideration when mating, whether you mate back-to-back litters or once a year.

It is wise to have your female examined by your vet to be certain she is in excellent health before breeding your next litter. If the vet determines she needs to rest and recover between litters, then this advice must be taken into serious consideration.

Shelby is in perfect health and ready to mate again soon

Chapter 11

What to Do if Things Go Wrong

Over 90% of litters are whelped without difficulties, but there's still about a 10% chance something could go wrong. It is an unpleasant fact that not all puppies will survive and large breeds, such as the German shepherd, tend to have fewer problems delivering puppies. It is still best to be informed and prepared beforehand on what to do in the event of an emergency. I have never had a whelping emergency but was always prepared for potential, common delivery problems that could lead to a life-threatening situation for the dam or the puppies. Common delivery problems include:

- **Puppy not breathing upon delivery**: After the mother tears and removes the placental sack and the puppy is not breathing, you need to act quickly to save the puppy. Remove any mucous, membrane, or other obstructions from the muzzle using the infant nasal aspirator, and perform CPR by placing your mouth over the puppy's nose and mouth and puff two breaths into the puppy till you see the stomach inflate slightly, follow by a gentle chest massage, and repeat with breathing and massaging until the puppy begins to breathe on its own. Generally this works quickly, and the puppy gasps for air almost immediately.

- **Puppy stuck in the birth canal**: This can be a dangerous situation for the puppy, dam, and any other unborn puppies, and you must intervene. If the puppy is visible in the birth canal, then generously lube your hands with KY Jelly and gently try to rotate him/her out.

- **Breech puppy**: If one is coming out legs first, then you must assist with removing it. Generously lube your hands with KY Jelly and gently pull it out.

- **Two puppies stuck in the birth canal**: If the dam is struggling with this situation then you must assist by lubing your hands with KY Jelly and then gently push one back into the mother to make room for the other one to come out. In this case, you may need to assist by rotating it out quickly so the next one can be safely delivered.

- Do you need to call the vet for help? Sometimes, trust your instincts and call the vet immediately if you see signs of something going significantly wrong. The dam will experience bleeding, but if you see excessive and continuous bleeding by the dam then something is wrong. Foul-smelling green vaginal discharge can indicate something is wrong. Extended laboring with no puppies being born requires immediate medical attention where it is possible that a caesarean section may need to be done. Signs of distress, pain, or lethargy in the dam such as hyperventilation, a rapid pulse, or perhaps a weak pulse will require immediate medical attention.

- If the dam is not lactating then she may have Eclampsia, also known as "milk fever." The puppies need to begin nursing immediately for survival and if the dam is not producing milk, she may need to go to the vet immediately to receive intravenous calcium supplementation. To avoid this situation, be certain the dam receives adequate amounts of calcium while pregnant. If there is an indication of Eclampsia, you will need to hand-feed the newborns until the mother is producing milk.

- If you have a weak newborn that is not nursing, you have to hand feed nutritional supplements using a baby bottle as described in the supplies to have available. Do not feed a puppy cow's milk. Their bodies cannot digest it, and it causes diarrhea, which can cause rapid dehydration and be fatal to a newborn. They consist of 85% water and can easily dehydrate. Prepare formula for them by mixing an 8-ounce container of vanilla yogurt, 1 can of evaporated milk (not low fat), 2 egg yolks, 6 ounces of boiled and then cooled water, and 2 drops of infant vitamins. Feed the formula at room temperature and store unused portion in the refrigerator. By holding one as if it were naturally nursing from the mother, you will promote suckling action. Do not cradle them on their backs while feeding to avoid asphyxiation. Only use the syringe to feed if the weak one cannot suckle. Feed very small amounts of formula at a time, feed them every 15 minutes using the syringe until he/she gains strength, and can be bottle-fed.

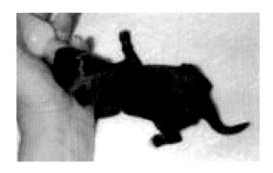

This is the proper technique for hand feeding using a bottle:

 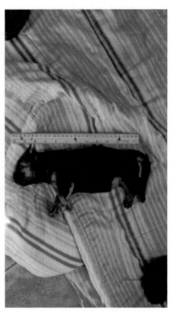

Chapter 12

Whelping Pen Design

There are many whelping pens available on the market today that you could simply assemble in your home. Or you could make your own. Lucky for me, my husband can build just about anything. He built our whelping pen using ¼"plywood. It measures 9' long by 7' wide. When the puppies are newborn, the pen does seem large, but as the puppies grow, it's going to get crowded. A pen this size is perfect. It is very comfortable for the mother to whelp her puppies and to nurse them. The pen must be built sturdy to be safe. When the puppies begin to walk and run, thrash and tumble around, they will be making such a ruckus. You definitely need a dependable and safe confinement for their well-being. The floor of the pen should be a washable surface so you can properly sanitize it. The door to enter the pen should be able to open and close quickly with ease and have a secure latch on the outside. They become fast to the exit very quickly. You will discover that once the puppies realize this is the "out" door when you begin to take them outdoors, they will try their earnest to escape at every given opportunity. The walls of the pen should be 4' tall, the standard measurement of a sheet of plywood.

You should avoid constructing your whelping pen using flake board, commonly called particle board or OSB board, because those products can sliver and splinter making it an unsafe material for the puppies.

The height of 4' may seem too tall, but we found that it makes for a safer height more for the mother than the puppies. We found that the mother would randomly try to jump into the pen, which could injure herself or her puppies. We want to be able to let the mother in and out of the pen to avoid a possible fatality to a puppy by being jumped on.

Part of the whelping pen design includes a movable partition that will create a paper-training area where the puppies will void. This partition should be placed at the furthest part of the pen away from the door. You want to partition the potty area from the rest of the pen so they do not run and play on the soiled papers when they are roughhousing around. The partition should be placed in such a way that fully opened sheets of newspaper fit perfectly in the space. We make this a movable partition for proper and thorough sanitizing.

The opposite side of the whelping pen, near the door, should be a secure wall built to provide a nesting and sleeping area for use when the puppies are older, around 3 to 4 weeks in age. The size we found works best measures roughly 4' long by 3' wide.

With blankets on the floor, they will find this to be a safe, cozy area, and they are most likely not going to void in an area where they sleep. The communal area between the paper training area and bedding area provides ample space for whelping, nursing, playing, eating and tending to the newly-formed family.

During the first few weeks, the puppies will be nursing, bonding with their mother, and sleeping on blankets in the communal area.

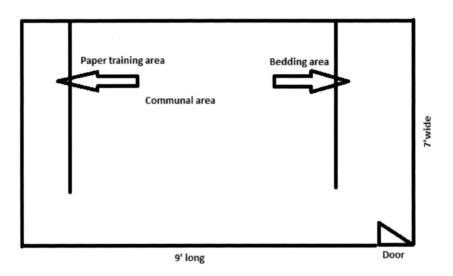

Paper training area   Communal area   Bedding area

Chapter 13

Paper-Training Tips

By the beginning of Week 4 you will be introducing the puppies to solid food. The same day they begin solid food is the same day paper-training begins. I have always had great success with paper training at this early age. German shepherd puppies are very intelligent and learn the concept rather quickly. For the next few days, you must remain diligent with this training process to achieve positive results. Begin by layering newspapers in the area. Carry one at a time to the area and set him/her down on the paper. Stay there until the puppy voids. Praise him/her then repeat the process until everyone has their poppy break. Do not remove the soiled papers. Place another layer of clean papers on top of the soiled ones. You want the urine and fecal scent to draw them to the papers to do their business. For the first few days, continue to add clean papers on top of soiled papers and on day four, you can remove all the soiled papers, sanitize the area, and start the process all over.

One effective method I found that works best is to wake up the puppies and place them on the papers. They always need to void the moment they wake up. So by you carrying them to the papers, they'll quickly pick up on the idea that this is what they should do. I had one litter that amazed me with the speed in which they noticed paper-training, and within just two days the entire litter was voiding on the papers. Another tip to share: you will have random accidents, and a puppy will void in the communal area, which you do not want to encourage. Instead of using paper towels to clean up this mess, use your newspapers. Cut a stack of newspapers into sheets the size of paper towels and keep them handy near the whelping pen. This tip will save you money, and it works just fine. Once solid food is introduced into the pups' diet, you need to stay on top of keeping the whelping pen sanitized all through the day and night. This is paramount in keeping your puppies as healthy as possible. I find that by keeping a mop and bucket of bleach water just outside the pen helps make cleaning up easier.

As the puppies grow, around Week 5, wake them and get them outside right away. This is the beginning of training the puppies to void outdoors. It is not possible to

84

completely housebreak a puppy while they are in your care, but this is a great starting point before they are adopted and move to their forever homes.

Paper training starts when the pups are four-weeks-old: The size of the paper training area is designed to fit a full sheet of newspaper

Chapter 14

Customer Testimonials

Virginia Clark is passionate about German shepherd Dogs; documenting each litter, from birth throughout the time one leaves with his or her chosen puppy.

She is well-educated and concerned with the puppies' health and well-being, nurturing the puppies all along the way. As they age and develop, she even teaches them how to sit and become well-mannered in the kitchen while waiting for their food. Such work and connection with each puppy in a litter is most impressive.

The parents of our puppy, Shelby and Duke, were on-site, clean, healthy and beautiful, having friendly temperaments; and, as a result, we took home a clean, happy and healthy puppy.

At that time, Virginia also provided us with the AKC paperwork, as well as the vet records.

My husband and I strongly recommend anyone looking for a German shepherd pup to contact Virginia, as well as to read and watch her blog. You will be most amazed. She takes such pride in making certain the puppies are clean, healthy and happy, and goes the extra mile by thoroughly documenting the puppies' development.

Thank you so much, Virginia, for allowing us to bring a healthy and happy German shepherd dog into our family!

Jim and Lisa C.
Henderson, Nevada

Teddy

We feel so fortunate to have stumbled across Virginia's blog when our family was looking for a puppy this summer. We highly recommend anyone who is considering becoming a puppy parent to contact Virginia -- she devotes herself to providing a solid, loving start to the litters she breeds.

Virginia's love for her own dogs, Duke and Shelby, and concern for their health and welfare was apparent immediately when we met. Her home was very clean, and the puppies were very well-cared for. All of the puppies we met had great dispositions, and had obviously been handled lovingly so they were not afraid of people. We were fortunate to get two puppies from her super-moon litter, and I cannot thank Virginia enough to getting our dogs off to a great start! She had started paper-training the puppies while they were still in her care, which made potty training so easy at home! Virginia is a responsible, ethical, organized breeder, and all of our AKC paperwork was explained to us and was ready when we picked up our pups.

Our puppies are gorgeous, healthy, intelligent, obedient and happy. We feel blessed to have found Virginia, and we encourage anyone who is planning to add a German shepherd to their family to check out Virginia's blog and highly recommend purchasing your puppy from her. You will be so happy you did!

Thanks again, Virginia!
Diana, Karl & Nick P.
Henderson, Nevada

Luna and Shadow

Their puppies are raised with lots of love and care. If you've been searching for a German shepherd puppy these are awesome breeders. We had a wonderful experience with the last litter.
Sheryl P
Henderson, NV

Nikita

Kaiser is doing great and playing nonstop with our other dog and son. He is the sweetest little guy ever. We love him so much. Thank you for taking such wonderful care of them. I have no doubt you are the reason he's such a great dog.
Amanda D
Las Vegas, NV

Kaiser

Virginia Clark is the most caring breeder I have ever met. From the moment we contacted her to the moment we brought our GSD home she has been nothing but professional and caring. The greatest part of getting our dog from Virginia is the fact that you can see your dog grow every day when she posts videos and pictures from the whelp day to the day you bring your puppy home on her puppy blog. This is an added bonus as the dogs come with AKC certified documents and shot records. If you are thinking of getting a GSD then look no more. This will be the greatest decision that you have made for the new addition to your family.

LaToya and Tom
Las Vegas, NV

Lana

They turn out great!
Eric S
Las Vegas, NV

Loki

Virginia is a wonderful breeder, her dogs are very well tempered and "pampered." She treats every pup of every litter as if they were the only pup. She delivers on her promises and is very nice to work with.

Erik and Stefani M
Las Vegas, NV

Doug

Just wanted to give you a lil' update on Stark! He is probably the best dog we've ever had! He's so gentle with our three-year-old and plays really well with our other dogs. Buying him from you was one of the best choices we've ever made! Every day I see the new lil' ones you post on here reminds me of when he was that little! Crazy how time flies!! Ha, but I just wanted to let you know he's doing great, and we love him so much! Thank you again!

Courtney C.
Las Vegas, NV

Stark

Chapter 15

Glossary

American Kennel Club, AKC:
The registry of purebred dog pedigrees in the United States.

Amniotic membrane:
The thin transparent membrane that holds a developing fetus.

Bulbus glands:
The bulb of the dog's penis which enlarges during an erection to prevent withdraw during an erection.

Dam:
 Describes the female parent: it is used on registration papers and pedigrees.

Eclampsia:
A toxemia that can occur during or immediately after pregnancy causing comas and convulsions.

Elbow dysplasia:
A condition involving multiple developmental abnormalities of the elbow-joint in the dog, specifically the growth of cartilage or the structures surrounding it.

Estrus:
Also known as a heat: It is the period of maximum sexual receptivity of the female.

Guerilla Marketing: An unconventional system of promotion that relies on patience, energy, and imagination rather than a big **advertising budget.**

 Hip dysplasia:
An abnormal formation of the hip socket that, in its more severe form, can eventually cause crippling lameness and painful arthritis of the joints.

Hypothermia:
Hypothermia is a medical condition that is characterized by an abnormally low body temperature.

Limited registration:
When a breeder requires you to spay or neuter the puppy you acquire from them.

Nesting behavior:
A behavior seen in pregnant females that are close to the time of whelping, where the female prepares a space to whelp.

Neuter:
The removal of testicles.

OFA numbers:
Orthopedic Foundation for Animals (OFA) is the organization that maintains a registry of hip dysplasia where dogs are assigned OFA numbers if they are certified free of canine hip dysplasia.

Pedigree:
The written genealogy that documents at least three generations of the dog's ancestry.

Shiver reflex:
When a puppy is able to regulate their own body heat and keep themselves warm at 3 weeks of age.

Sire:
Describes the male parent: It is used on registration papers and pedigrees.

Spay:
The removal of uterus and ovaries.

Tie:
The pairing of male and female in reproduction.

Whelping:
To give birth.

Conclusion

During their successful breeding career, Shelby and Duke gave birth to forty-four puppies. Unfortunately, four of their puppies did not survive. Sadly, it happens. The remaining forty were perfect in every way. I have met so many wonderful people along the way, and our babies have brought great joy to those forty families who adopted them. Endearing to my heart, it was such a rewarding experience breeding Shelby and Duke and by documenting the journey of all their family, I fondly look back on all the pictures and videos I posted on my social networking sites. It was an afterthought that the documentation has become invaluable to me as I relive the days when all of them were in my care. A piece of my heart went home with each puppy.

I knew the day would eventually arrive to retire Shelby. I have always kept her best interests and health a top priority, above breeding. This includes having her spayed and ending her breeding career when the time was right. Well, that day did come, and today Shelby has been spayed and is finished breeding. Now her job is to just be my gentle, affectionate best girl, and she loves that role quite a bit. It was heart wrenching for me to leave her at the vet for her spay operation, but I knew it was the right thing to do.

Selfishly, I wanted more puppies with Shelby and Duke because the joy is so tremendous that I did not want the experience to end so soon. Therefore, I planned ahead, and bought another female that I named Gia. She recently came into estrus, and I bred her with Duke. I am looking forward to taking another step on the breeding journey.

I welcome your feedback, and if you have breeding questions, I encourage you to contact me. I have accumulated a great deal of knowledge and experience over the years and may be able to help answer your questions. I also encourage you to join my social networking sites to view the collections of documentation on all our puppies and to see future updates with Gia and Duke.

"A complete guide to breeding healthy puppies from an experienced, caring breeder. It is very thorough, yet concise and very readable."

Judy Van Der Walt, DVM
Henderson Animal Hospital
Henderson, Nevada

Here are more visuals for you. I hope you love them as much as I enjoyed making and living them with my babies:

Slideshow compilation from documenting the journey from birth through adoption

https://www.youtube.com/watch?v=Vg5__xdYjh0

MY FAVORITE VIDEO! We call this "The running of the bulls" with the pups going out!

https://www.youtube.com/watch?v=W-nowgTb8AI

Virginia Clark

After suffering through decades of long, seemingly endless, harsh winters in Buffalo, New York, Virginia Clark, and her husband Robert, decided it was time to relocate to someplace warm and sunny. They wanted to live in a place that was more conducive to breeding their dogs. Packing the meager-less of items, they moved to Henderson, Nevada with their two grown German shepherds, Duke and Shelby.

Once situated in their new home, Virginia resumed her successful 10 year breeding career. She quickly found a vast following of people in Nevada who became interested in adopting her puppies. Virginia knew she would find a warmer climate to work to her advantage because the pups could spend more time outdoors once they were old enough to venture out; an activity hindered by the cold climate in Buffalo, New York. Socializing and training her pups outdoors before adoption is a priority.

Virginia documents the journey of her pups' life daily, from birth through adoption, via pictures and videos on her blog and Facebook page for everyone to see. During her successful breeding career, she has acquired vast knowledge of caring for puppies, and many other breeds of dogs, besides German shepherds. She is often asked questions from people on how to properly care for their new pup and how to care for them as they mature into adult dogs. Virginia is also called upon to consult other breeders and to assist them with finding good families to adopt their puppies.

As more and more people recognized her talents as a reputable breeder, Virginia decided it was time to document her experiences and share with others the valuable information she has learned over the years. Her first book, *A Guide to Puppy Love; Beginner Breeding* was released in 2015 and won the 2016 Book Excellence Award for its quality and content. She penned her second book, *A Puppy Love Day; Tips for Bringing a New Puppy Home* which is also award winning. Virginia is now compiling a series of ten books on the most popular dogs in America according to the American Kennel Association. Virginia Clark's books are represented by the highly regarded author and publisher Joyce Foy at A Vegas Publisher.

Books by Virginia Clark

Award Winning *A Guide to Puppy Love; Beginner Breeding*

Award Winning *A Puppy Love Day; Tips for Bringing Your New Puppy Home*

A Puppy Love Guide; About the Labrador Retriever, Tips for Bringing Your Lab Puppy Home, and Doggone Delicious Recipes

A Puppy Love Guide; About the German Shepherd, Tips for Bringing your GSD Pup Home, and Doggone Delicious Recipes

A Puppy Love Guide; About the Golden Retriever, Tips for Bringing your Golden Pup Home, and Doggone Delicious Recipes!

Award Winning *Blitz Your Book to a Best Seller 21st Century* written by Joyce Spizer Foy and Virginia Clark

82282816R00058

Made in the USA
Lexington, KY
28 February 2018